START-UP
DESIGN AND TECHNOLOGY

HOUSES AND HOMES

Louise and Richard Spilsbury

Evans

Published by Evans Brothers Limited
2A Portman Mansions
Chiltern Street
London W1U 6NR

© Evans Brothers Limited 2006

Produced for Evans Brothers Limited by
White-Thomson Publishing Ltd.,
Bridgewater Business Centre, 210 High Street,
Lewes, East Sussex BN7 2NH

Printed in China by WKT Company Limited

Editor: Dereen Taylor
Consultants: Nina Siddall, Head of Primary School
Improvement, East Sussex; Norah Granger, former
primary head teacher and senior lecturer in Education,
University of Brighton
Designer: Leishman Design

The right of Louise and Richard Spilsbury to be
identified as the authors of this work has been asserted
by them in accordance with the Copyright, Designs and
Patents Act 1988.

British Library Cataloguing in Publication Data
Spilsbury, Louise
    Houses and Homes - (Start-up design
    and technology)
    1. Architecture, Domestic - Juvenile literature
    2. Dwellings
    I. Title II. Spilsbury, Louise
    728

ISBN: 0 237 53025 2
13-digit ISBN (from 1 Jan 2007) 978 0 237 53025 9

Acknowledgements:
Special thanks to the following for their help and
involvement in the preparation of this book:
Staff and pupils at Coldean Primary School, Brighton;
Elm Grove Primary School, Brighton and
Hassocks Infants School, Hassocks.

Picture Acknowledgements:
Chris Fairclough cover, 5 (right), 8, 9, 12 (right), 13, 14,
15, 19, 20, 21; Corbis 16, 17; Ecoscene 4 (bottom right);
Liz Price title page, 5 (left), 10, 11, 12 (left); Topfoto 7;
WTpix 4 (top and bottom left).

Artwork:
Emily Price age 5, page 6 (right); Tom Price age 8,
page 6 (left); Hattie Spilsbury age 10, pages 13 and 18.

Contents

Houses and homes

Jack's class is looking at different kinds of homes. There are terraced houses, blocks of flats, and detached houses near Jack's school.

What is the purpose of houses and homes?
Why do houses come in different designs?

     homes   terraced   houses   flats

"We live in a block of flats. Our flat is on the top floor."

"There's a house on either side of my terraced house."

What kind of home do you live in?

detached   purpose   designs

Outside and inside

Asha lives in an old cottage. Jess lives in a new terraced house. They have drawn pictures of their homes with labels for the different features.

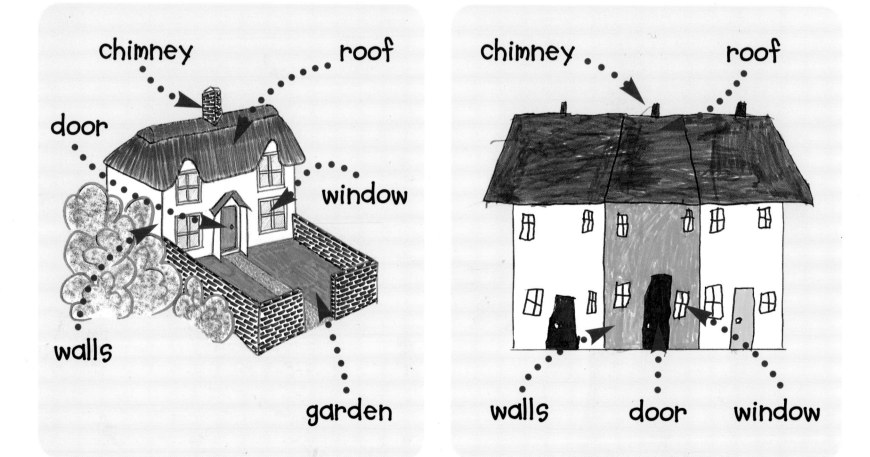

How are the houses similar? How are they different?

cottage   labels   features

Can you match the words around the picture to the correct rooms in this doll's house?

bathroom   kitchen   hall

lounge   bedroom   dining room

Is it a model of an old house or a new house?
What rooms does your home have?

similar   rooms   7

Shapes and homes

Stefan drew a picture of his house on the computer.

He used the mouse to move different shapes across the screen. He made a house from circles, squares, rectangles and triangles.

computer   mouse

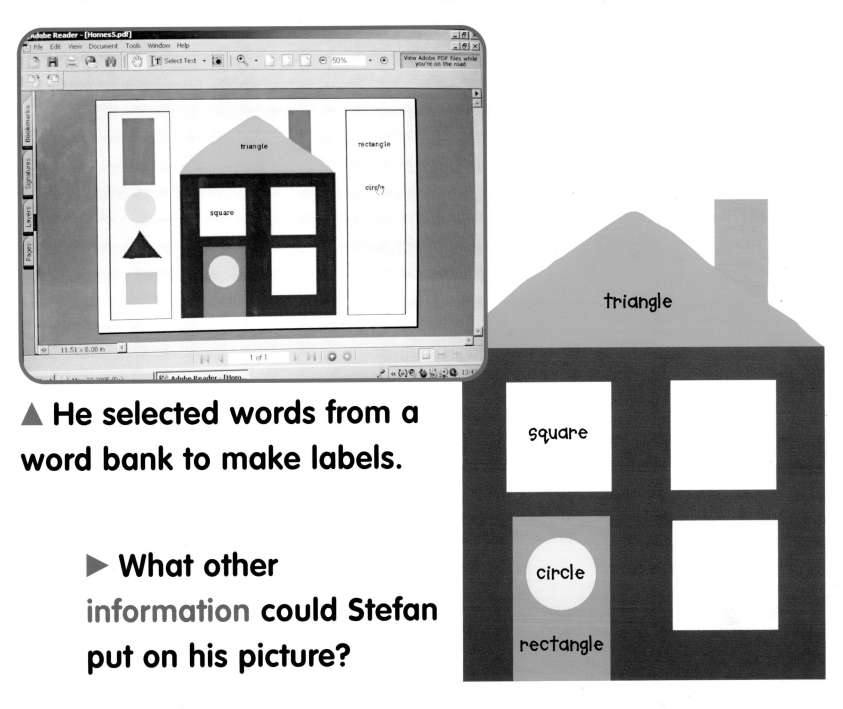

▲ He selected words from a word bank to make labels.

▶ What other information could Stefan put on his picture?

What kind of house would you make from shapes? Who would you design a house for?

screen   information

Making a house

Emily has been reading 'The Three Little Pigs'. She wants to make a **strong model** house for the pigs.

Would you make a **flat** roof with Lego boards like Emily, or a **steep** roof from folded cardboard?

strong   **model**   **flat**   **steep**

Emily tests her house.

▲ She rests a book on top to check the roof won't fall in.

▲ Emily's grandpa uses a hairdryer to check it won't blow down.

How can Emily test if the house is waterproof?

test   waterproof

Materials hunt

Emily looks at different materials in her home.

▲ The windows are made of glass. Glass is transparent.

▲ The roof is covered with stone tiles. They keep the rain out.

materials   glass   transparent

▼ **The front door is made of wood. Wood is strong.**

133

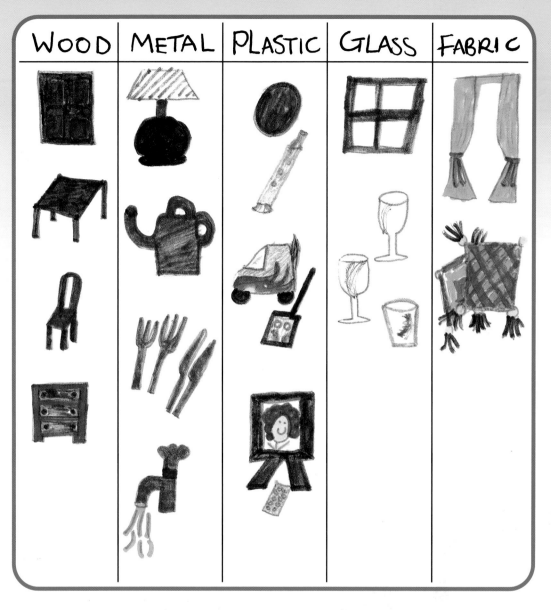

WOOD	METAL	PLASTIC	GLASS	FABRIC

▲ **Emily made a chart to group the different materials in her home. What other objects in your home could you add to this chart?**

stone   tiles   wood

Designing a bedroom

Tamika is making a bedroom for her dolls.

▲ Tamika writes a list of things that could go in the bedroom.

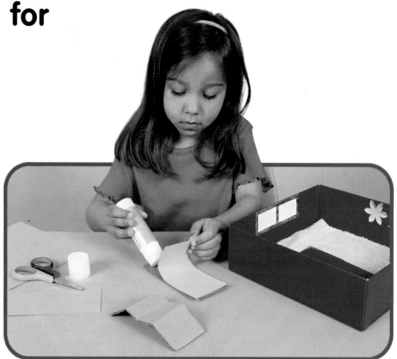

▲ She uses a box for her room and puts soft carpet on the floor. Tamika glues together two layers of card to make the table.

Why does Tamika use two layers of card for her table?

soft   glues

Materials and tools
- scissors • glue • foil • carpet sample • fabric • dolls • carboard box • yogurt pot • card • pens

◄ **Tamika chooses the doll that is the right scale for the room.**

WARNING!
Scissors are sharp.
Use them with care.

How could Tamika improve the bedroom? What kind of bedroom would you design for your best friend?

scale   improve   15

Homes around the world

Hassan's class is looking at homes around the world.

◀ White walls keep homes cool in hot places.

▶ Steep roofs let melting snow slide off homes in cold places.

◄ **Why is this house on stilts?**

► **An architect designs buildings. The model is small but everything on it is built to scale.**

Why would an architect make a model like this?

stilts   architect   buildings   **17**

Planning a model house

Josie is planning a model bungalow for her grandpa who cannot climb stairs. She draws her design and thinks about the materials she will use.

card shapes for tiles

plastic container for windows

hinge

fabric for curtains

split pin for door handle

Why do you think she chooses a split pin for the door handle?

bungalow   split pin

Josie tests different ways of making hinges for the door.

▲ She scores and bends card to make a hinge.

◄ She joins two pieces of card together with tape.

scores   bends   hinges   19

Making a model house

▲ Josie opens a cardboard box and cuts two windows. Then she cuts and bends the door.

▲ She sticks in the windows and the curtains.

▲ She sticks the box back together. Then she folds a piece of card for the roof and checks that it fits.

fits   decorated   evaluate

Josie has decorated her house. She asks Ben to evaluate her model.

The transparent windows work really well and I like the opening door.

Materials and tools
- cardboard box • paint • fabric
- coloured card • scissors • glue
- plastic container • split pin

Do you think Josie's house looks like her plan? Why do you think this is?

Further information for

Possible Activities

PAGES 4–5

Children could go on a walk to find out what different kinds of buildings are near their school. You could take photographs and make a labelled display of the different types of houses they see. Children could also make a simple pictorial map of their route showing where the houses are located.

Children could make a class chart or pictogram showing the kinds of houses the children live in to see which is the most common type of home in their area.

PAGES 6–7

The children could make drawings of other buildings such as a garden shed, playhouse, barn or skyscraper.

Children could play a guessing game with a selection of photographs of different types of homes. One child chooses two words from a prepared list (old, new, detached, terraced, etc.) to describe a house and another child has to guess which home they are describing.

PAGES 8–9

Children could make a collage of a building using shape stickers. They could label the shapes and the parts of the houses they represent.

Children could use a painting program or clip art on the computer to design a real or fantasy room or house for themselves or another person.

PAGES 10–11

Discuss other ways of testing Emily's house, and how to make sure the tests are safe.

The class could read Jill Murphy's 'On the Way Home' and talk about why school is different to home and why we need homes.

PAGES 12–13

Using a wordbank children could select words (such as bendy/not bendy, transparent/not transparent) to describe common materials used in their homes.

Children could be given a list of parts for a model building, such as window, door, carpet, table, and be asked to select the

Parents and Teachers

most appropriate material for each from a variety of reclaimed materials and explain their choice.

PAGES 14–15

The children could add lots of different decorative features to a room they make, perhaps with a specific purpose or theme, such as paper chains for a Christmas scene. Ask the children to evaluate their own and each other's rooms.

The children could make household items that they can really use in their homes, such as a photo frame (for making hinges see pages 18-19) or a fridge magnet.

PAGES 16–17

Children could look at houses in the past. Some houses were built a long time ago. How are they similar to modern houses? How are they different? What different things would you have found in their rooms long ago?

Children could look at pictures of unusual buildings around the world, such as igloos, yurts and log cabins. Then they could discuss the fact that today improved transport means many buildings across the world are made from similar materials, whereas in the past people had to use materials that were easily available.

PAGES 18–19

Children could design a house for a specific person with particular requirements.

When making and using hinged doors or windows the children could think about the push and pull forces involved.

Further Information

BOOKS FOR CHILDREN

Home (Around the World) by Margaret Hall (Heinemann Library, 2003)

Homes (Start-up History) by Stewart Ross (Evans, 2004)

Homes (Starters) by Rosie McCormick (Hodder Children's Books, 2003)

Homes (Toppers) by Nicola Baxter (Franklin Watts, 2003)

Materials (Start-up Science) by Claire Llewellyn (Evans, 2004)

Where We Live (In Your Neighbourhood) by Sally Hewitt (Franklin Watts, 2004)

WEBSITES

www.constructionawards.co.uk/house/index.php

www.eriding.net/dandt/index.shtml

www.primaryresources.co.uk/art/art.html

PAGES 20–21

When the children have made a model they could make a list of what worked well and what they like about their finished home, and which parts might have been better and how. They could also assess each other's work.

Index